THE PRACTICE

OF

Manœuvring

A

Battalion of INFANTRY.

By WILLIAM YOUNG,

Late MAJOR of BRIGADE to the Corps of
GRENADIERS and HIGHLANDERS who
ferved in *Germany*, and now in
the fervice of *Brunfwick*.

The Naval & Military Press Ltd

Published by
The Naval & Military Press Ltd
Unit 10 Ridgewood Industrial Park,
Uckfield, East Sussex,
TN22 5QE England
Tel: +44 (0) 1825 749494
Fax: +44 (0) 1825 765701
www.naval-military-press.com

The Naval & Military Press

MILITARY HISTORY AT YOUR FINGERTIPS

... a unique and expanding series of reference works

Working in collaboration with the foremost regiments and institutions, as well as acknowledged experts in their field, N&MP have assembled a formidable array of titles including technologically advanced CD-ROMs and facsimile reprints of impossible-to-find rarities.

In reprinting in facsimile from the original, any imperfections are inevitably reproduced and the quality may fall short of modern type and cartographic standards.

On the Thiev—ng Pirateers of the ARMY LIST; and their worse greedy, sculking, insidious, lame Helpers, Abettors, &c. who, by Omissions, &c. have above 1000 Errors in theirs for 1770.

THE War-Office List bears the same Authority on any Occasion as their Commissions——whereas a Piracy can have no Authority.——The Attempt is the most inviduous Invasion on Property and Trade. Can they be less guilty than a Den of common Thieves?

Soon may be published,

1. The SCANDALOUS REGISTER, of the Filchean Shylockean Crew of Piratical-Booksellers, the Disgrace of Trade and Society, *viz.* Crowderian, M'Robin, M'Robert, J. and T. Curs'm, Old Nick, Puggy H——wes, Culley, Clericus, M'Richards and Urquhartionian Den of cowardly———to rob a Man old enough to be Grandfather to the oldest of them, yet able to give the whole Crew a fatherly Correction, and teach them, and their dirty sculking Helpers, the Manœuvre of the Nose jig Dance, and turn them into Foot-balls, but scorns to attack what is so infinitely inferior to him, who in the Course of about 60 Years Trade has not given the least offence.

These are *your Liberty and Property!*——London Booksellers, Fomenters of Defamation, Sedition, Treason, and Blasphemy, the Grave of Liberty!

With the same Concience they would strip Mankind, their best Customers, and even one another. By means of such Desperadoes, the Liberty and Commerce of most Nations have suffered.

The hang-in-chains-looking Filche's highest Ambition is in declaring himself a Traitor, an Atheist, &c. as most of his Gang may, who regard no Honour, Honesty, Religion, Profession, or Property, &c.

One of this hopeless Crew, in his Remorse, has concluded with a Piracy upon Esq; Ketch, as I fear the rest and their paultry Helpers will.———They who rob the Rich, would rob the Poor, he who wrongs his Enemy, would his Father.

Few Robbers on Resistance, but would Kill; these Wretches make a jest of hanging, the greatest Villain should never be deprived of Life; set them to all the obnoxious hard Labours, 16 hours a Day, spare Diet, no Women to come in sight of the Men, or Men in the Apartments of the Women, chained and badged, evey part of their Apparel, so as to denote their various Crimes; Murders and House breakers, with a Death's Head, labelled, thou shalt not kill; Piratical Booksellers, a Wooden-book clog, chained to their Legs, labelled, Thou shalt not steal, &c.——— By these Means, thousands would become useful to the Community, and millions deterr'd from their more dreaded Destiny than a thousand DEATHS.

To His Royal Highness
WILLIAM Duke of *Gloucester*,

Lieutenant-General of His Majesty's Land Forces, &c.

IF intending well, can claim any share of the merit of performing well, this short treatise on Military Manœuvres may hope for the Approbation of your royal highness, the surest road to whose protection is an endeavour both in theory and practice, to render the Profession of a soldier at the same time useful and intelligible. Whatever may be thought of this performance, there is nothing, I am more certain of, than that my intention is to give a testimony of my anxiety to deserve your royal highness's countenance, and to prove with how much respect,

I am,

Your royal highness's,

Most devoted

Most obedient

And most humble Servant,

St. Vincents,
March 4, 1770.

WILLIAM YOUNG.

To Mr. MILLAN.

St. Vincent, March 4, 1770.

SIR,

HAVING had time during the voyage to compose a small treatise upon the PRACTICE of manœuvring of troops, upon the same principles, with those you published for me under the title of MANOEUVRES FOR A BATTALION OF INFANTRY, BY A GERMAN OFFICER, I send you this treatise: As I think the TABLE OF MANOEUVRES is now put into such a form as will answer almost every situation a battalion should be in, and a method is proposed, which if often practiced by young officers, may be very conducive to qualify them, not only to manœuvre battalions; but likewise to serve as ASSISTANTS, to the adjutant and quarter master general, or their deputies when employed as such; particularly if they accustom themselves to sketch in the manner mentioned, the marches and journies they make in the country, and apply to them the proper manœuvres; I venture to put my name to this small treatise, relying upon your usual care in preventing the errors of the press and of engraving.

I am,

SIR,

Your most obedient servant,

W. YOUNG.

(5)

B **TABLE I. of Manœuvres.** C

B   G

1. Battal.   from the { right / left / centre / flanks } { advance / retire } by { Ind. Files. 1. / Files. 2. / Platoons. 3. / Sub Divis. 4. }

2. Wings!   to the { right / left } change the front. 5.

3. G Div.   on the centre to the { right. 6. / left. 7. } change the front.

4. S. Div.   form the { square / oblong / 2 deep } { advancing. 8. / retiring. 9. / on the march. 10. }

5. Platoons!

6. Columns!   Take ground to the { right. 11. / left. 12. }

William Young, Inv.

B   C

TABLE II. of Manœuvres, FORMING.

1. Platoons!
2. S. } Div.   to the { right / left } { form the / change the } Front. 5.   { Battal. 1. / Wings. 2. / G. Div. 3. / S. Div. 4. }
3. G. }
4. Wings!

Grenada, March 1, 1770.

EXPLANATION of the foregoing TABLE.

SUPPOSE a battalion is to march into a country by two different roads, each of which will admit of six men in front; or that they are to pass a river in which are two fords only. It is evident that the battalion must pass it in two columns, which must advance from their centres, that the battalion may more easily be formed, when the manœuvre is to be compleated. Therefore look into the left hand side of the table marked B, and you will find No. 2 opposite the first word of the manœuvre, and figure 2 under C, opposite to the last; The first is WINGS and the last is FILES. These two words cannot be filled up, so as to make sense, with any of the intermediate words except these, FROM THE CENTRE ADVANCE BY FILES. Therefore the order to be given is,

WINGS! FROM THE CENTRE ADVANCE BY FILES.

The retreat for the same manœuvre, begins on the left under B, at figure 2, and likewise ends at figure 2, under C: But then it is,

Wings! from the FLANKS retire by files.

Had the roads only admitted of one man in front, The manœuvre would have been begun at 2 under B. and have ended at 1 under C that is,

Wings! from the right retire by Indian files.

Suppose there were four defiles to pass in front of the battalion. Look in the left hand of the table under B, marked 3. And you'll find the first word, GRAND DIVISIONS! and under the letter C at 2 BY FILES; therefore reading the intermediate words you have.

GRAND DIVISIONS! FROM THE RIGHT ADVANCE BY FILES.

And

And if it is necessary to march to the right, look for figure 6, under B. and you'll find the word *Columns!* and for figure 11 under C, where you'll find *right*; therefore the word is,

Columns! take ground to the right.

(From 1 B. to b. c. is the word)

Battalion on the centre to the right change the front.

And so on, to answer every situation.

Should it be necessary to march through a brush-wood country; look for figure 5 under B, and figure 1 under C, upon reading which you'll find,

Platoons! from the right advance by Indian files.

If it is proper to attack in columns with a grand division in front, look for figure 1 under B, and figure 4 under C, where you'll see the words to be read betwixt these two are,

Battalion! from the centre, advance by sub divisions.

And for the retreat of this manœuvre, betwixt the two figures is the word.

Battalion! from the flanks, retire by sub divisions.

Were it necessary upon account of two defiles, each of which would admit of a sub division to retire by, to form two Columns retreating. Look for figure 2, under B, and figure 3, under C, between which the words are.

Wings! from the flanks retire by platoons.

Should a battalion be so situated, that by the enemies approaching the left flank, it is obliged to throw itself into sub divisions in order to practice the street firing, look for figure 4, under B, and for figure 2 under C where you'll find.

Sub Divisions! from the right advance by files.

And should the enemy retire and the ground admit of two lines, look in table 2, for figure 2 under B, and for figure 2 under C where you read,

Sub Divisions! to the right form wings.

PREFACE

PREFACE.

THE manoeuvres of a battalion, are so various that they may be compared to the combinations of letters, whereby words are formed; or to the changes that may be rung on a set of bells, yet by disposing properly of words on a table, a few of them may by combination, answer every word of command, that can possibly be given with propriety; I have attempted this, in the annexed table, and though I may not have fully succeeded, yet other officers ought not to be discouraged in attempting it, for how trifling will this difficulty appear, when compared with those, which they who first formed troops had to encounter. What immense labour must have been bestowed by them in forming a RABBLE into simple lines, and in teaching them the method of moving uniformly therein! Even now, that by long experience, the armies of Europe ONLY, have arrived at that perfection; by what difficulties and labour have they attained it! a recruit of common genius after being many months at the drill is scarcely able to KEEP THE STEP! yet how insignificant is this, compared to the evolutions necessary to the movement of a battalion or army! where even the different positions of rising grounds, roads, hedges, rivers, bridges, woods, &c. make it necessary to vary the manoeuvre, the embarassments attending which, will still be magnified according to the *movement* of the enemy, whether he advances upon the right, left, front or rear.

Though

PREFACE.

Though the marches of armies, ftiled the GRAND MANOEUVERE; are regulated upon the very principles, which determine the movement of a battalion; yet no fyftem of manœuvres has yet been publifhed in Europe. I wifh the few hints I have given, may induce fome experienced officer, to compofe a more extenfive treatife upon the fubject, for the ufe of the army.

COMBINATION.

Of words of command for the firft table, from 6 figures under B, to 12 under C, with the words, right, left, fquare, oblong, and two deep; containing the number of manœuvres in that table.

From 1. B. to $\begin{Bmatrix} 1 \\ 2 \\ 3 \\ 4 \end{Bmatrix}$ C. is 1. Movement by Indian files

C. 1. to fall fr. the rt. adv. 4.
The fame retiring is - - - - 4.
total 8.

From the $\begin{Bmatrix} \text{left is} \\ \text{centre} \\ \text{flanks} \end{Bmatrix}$ - - - - 8.
- - - - 8.
- - - - 8.

From $\begin{Bmatrix} 1 \\ 2 \\ 3 \\ 4 \\ 5 \\ 6 \end{Bmatrix}$ B. to 1. 2. 3. 4. C. By $\begin{Bmatrix} \text{batt. total} & 32. \\ \text{wings} & 32. \\ \text{g. divifions} & 32. \\ \text{fub divifi.} & 24. \\ \text{platoons} & 16. \\ \text{columns} & 32. \end{Bmatrix}$

Manœuvres 168.

From

COMBINATION.

$$\text{From 1. 2. 3. 4. 5. 6. B to} \begin{cases} 5.\text{ C. to the} \begin{cases} \text{right is } 6. \\ \text{left is } 6. \end{cases} \\ 6.\text{ C. is } - - - 6. \\ 7.\text{ C. is } - - - 6. \\ \overline{\text{Manœuvres } 192.} \\ 8.\text{ C. is } - - 6. \end{cases}$$

$$\text{For} \begin{cases} \text{the oblong } - - 6. \\ \text{two deep } - - 6. \end{cases}$$

total 18.

to $\begin{cases} 9.\text{ C.} - - - 18. \\ 10.\text{ C.} - - - 18. \end{cases}$

$\overline{256}$

From 1. 2. 3. 4. 5. 6. B. to $\begin{cases} 11.\text{ C.} - - 6. \\ 12.\text{ C.} - - 6. \end{cases}$

This table contains manœuvres $\overline{268.}$

The Second TABLE for *Formings*.

From 1. 2. 3. 4. B. to $\begin{Bmatrix} 1. \\ 2. \\ 3. \\ 4. \end{Bmatrix}$ C. by the right $\begin{cases} 4. \\ 3. \\ 2. \\ 1. \end{cases}$

total $\overline{10.}$
by the left 10.
$\overline{20.}$

From 1. 2. 3. 4. B. to 5. C. - $\overline{4.}$

This table contains 24. different ways of forming.

MANŒUVRES.

N. B. It is proper to observe that the order to be given to the battalion, is always composed in such manner, that it begins with the *word* expressing the order it is in, for example; if the battalion is marching to the front by grand divisions

from

from the right in file, and it is necessary to attack in a column of a grand division in front, the leading files in marching must approach the point to be attacked, and the order should begin with the words, *grand divisions*, for to them you speak, therefore it is,

Grand divisions! to the right change the front!

Whereby the superfluous word, column, is avoided, which should only be used when the battalion is in columns.

Where *orders of march* are given to an army, the different bodies of troops are mentioned in them by name; If a small one, *regiments*; if a larger, *brigades*; and if such as made war in Germany, *corps*; which refer during the whole campaign to the *order of battle* composed at the beginning of it, and given out in publick orders for the staff to regulate all marches by. The *order of battle* is the base upon which is formed the superstructure of the *grand manœuvre*, and though it is altered by verbal orders in the day of battle, yet it remains the same with respect to marches, unless a new *order of battle* is given out in orders. As every company has its fixt place in a battalion, until any of them are altered by a *written order*, which may be called the base of their manœuvres; therefore the platoons, sub divisions, grand divisions, of a battalion may be looked upon as battalions, brigades, and corps of an army in miniature; the word given the one, should resemble the written orders of march given the other, which is the best method to avoid confusion, and the surest way to form an idea of the *grand manœuvre*. Therefore the order to a battalion should always begin with that word which expresses the order they are then marching in, whether platoons, sub divisions, wings, columns, or battalion.

The

The Small and Grand MANOEUVRE compared.

The small	The grand
a Platoon represents	a Battalion
4 make	4 make
a Grand division represents	a Brigade
2 make	2 make
a Wing represents	a Corps
2 make	2 make
a Battalion represents	an Army

THE PRACTICE
OF
Manœuvring, &c.

MANY young gentlemen, though well qualified to study the profession of arms, find in time of peace, great difficulties; particularly in the practical part of manœuvring of troops.

If they are not attached to a well diciplined corps, it is almost impossible for them to form any just idea of this part of their duty. And though they may have the good fortune to belong to a corps remarkable for its manœuvres and good dicipline; yet if such corps, is confined to a straitned garrison, there will not of course be opportunities to *vary* their *movements,* by applying them to the several situations, which in war, a regiment may find itself in.

To remedy these inconveniences, and in some measure to accustom the young gentlemen of the army to begin an early study of this subject, which at the same time may amuse them; I'll suppose a game at backgammon, or at chess, may give way to one less fashionable, though more useful.

Suppose one with a crayon, or piece of chalk, scratches, or to speak more methodically, sketches upon a table, part of a country, such as the specimen annexed, and *forms* thereupon a battalion of infantry, with ivory or leaden platoons, in such situations as he shall think most proper; posting his grenadiers as his fancy directs, and placing his artillery upon the most commanding ground.

He may then allow his antagonist to bring the RESEMBLANCE of another battalion to attack him, with artillery, grenadiers, and hussars, as they betwixt themselves shall agree; they then may fix upon the following regulations before they begin the attack and defence.

1st. No order is to be given but what would be practicable upon such ground as is represented on the table, that is to say, the battalion shall not be moved in *line* through a brushwood country; nor even any river but at such places as have been previously represented as fords or bridges.

2dly. That no order shall be supposed to be executed in less time than is required for the troops to march from one position to another, according to the scale annexed, allowing a sufficient time for the mounting of hills by artillery, &c.

3d. That a longer *movement* at one time shall not be made than what could have been executed before there was a possibility of his antagonist knowing of, and preventing such *movement*, by placing his troops upon the ground intended to be occupied, provided he chuses to take possession of it, which he is entitled to, if posted nearer to it.

4th. Every *movement*, in case of dispute, shall be measured by compass, and the annexed scale, allowing a mile only to be marched in an hour, to avoid large plans, and throwing away the odd yards, to make the hour more divisible.

Yards

$$\text{Yards} \begin{Bmatrix} 800 \\ 400 \\ 200 \\ 50 \end{Bmatrix} \text{in} \begin{Bmatrix} 32 \\ 16 \\ 8 \\ 2 \end{Bmatrix} \text{Minutes.}$$

Suppose then the length of a battalion 160 yards.

$$a \begin{Bmatrix} \text{platoon will be} & 10 \\ \text{sub division} & 20 \\ \text{grand division} & 40 \\ \text{wing} & 80 \end{Bmatrix} \text{yards}$$

And if a foot rule is chosen as a scale, and the leaden or ivory platoons are exactly half an inch long, eight inches marked upon the table will contain a battalion drawn up in line: so that upon a table of two feet square, three battalions may be manœuvred,

$$\text{upon} \begin{Bmatrix} 4 & - & 6 \\ 8 & - & 12 \\ 16 & - & 24 \end{Bmatrix}$$

And if it is necessary to manœuvre an army upon the table, then let each of the platoons represent battalions, and each of the leaden squadrons represent regiments of cavalry; then a table of 16 feet will contain a country of above 200 square miles, since half an inch will then be the scale of 160 yards.

5th. The victory shall be decided in favour of him who gains the other's flanks, and comes within musquet shot before he can change his position; or he who by having made choice of *inattackable* positions, forces his enemy to the edge of the table, and prevents his communication with the interior parts of the country.

EXAMPLE I, PLATE I.

The river Werra is sketched upon the table; from K. to A. and H. it is scarcely fordable, in presence of an enemy; but has a bridge at K.

the rising grounds at M. are inaccessable; there is a thick wood at L.

A battalion represented by 16 platoons, in ivory or lead, two platoons of grenadiers, two amusetts, and a squadron of hussars, are placed with their right at the wood L. and their left at the river Werra; while the antagonist is placing his troops along the river at A. intending to attack in flank, the manœuvre to be performed in order to avoid this attack, is taken from the first table of manœuvres marked II.

WORDS of COMMAND.

Grand divisions from the right advance by files.

Upon which, the right hand file of each grand division wheels out to the left, the rest follow successively, until the whole arrive upon the second position: when the battalion will appear in four columns; to make which more clear, the platoons should be numbered from right to left, so that if any of them be improperly wheeled, and put out of their position, it will immediately be observed; and if the numbers are put in the front of the platoons: should it have wheeled by the rear, in place of the front, et vice versa, the mistake may be immediately rectified.

N. B. These platoons, squadrons, artillery, &c. may be had at Mr. MILLAN's.

The battalion being now in four grand divisions, (see C. in the plate) it is ordered to front the enemy; and as the ground from the heights of M. to the bend of the Werra is too small to admit of the whole battalion in front, in order to oppose the passage of the enemy, it must be formed in two lines.

Grand Divisions! to the right form Wings.
(See 2d table, No. II.)

The

SCALE
Yards

Enemy's 1st Position
The Werra

G 1st Line intended H
G H
2d Line
C C
16 15 14 13
C
12 11 10 9
C
8 7 6 5
C
4 3 2 1

Grenadiers

The Werra

The Enemy's second Position along here.

Practicable Ground

Hussars E
Hussars
Hussars
Hussars

Third Position

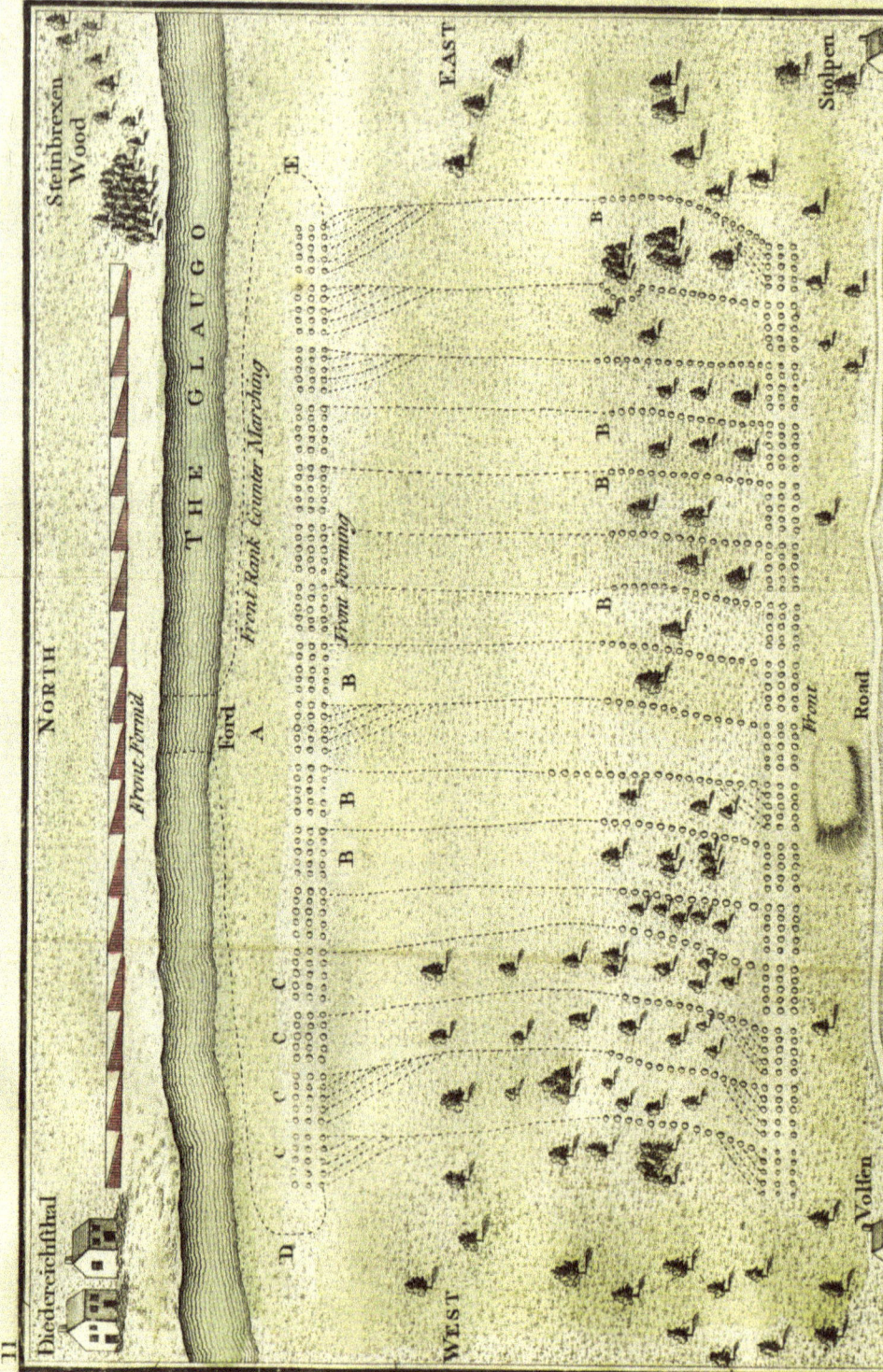

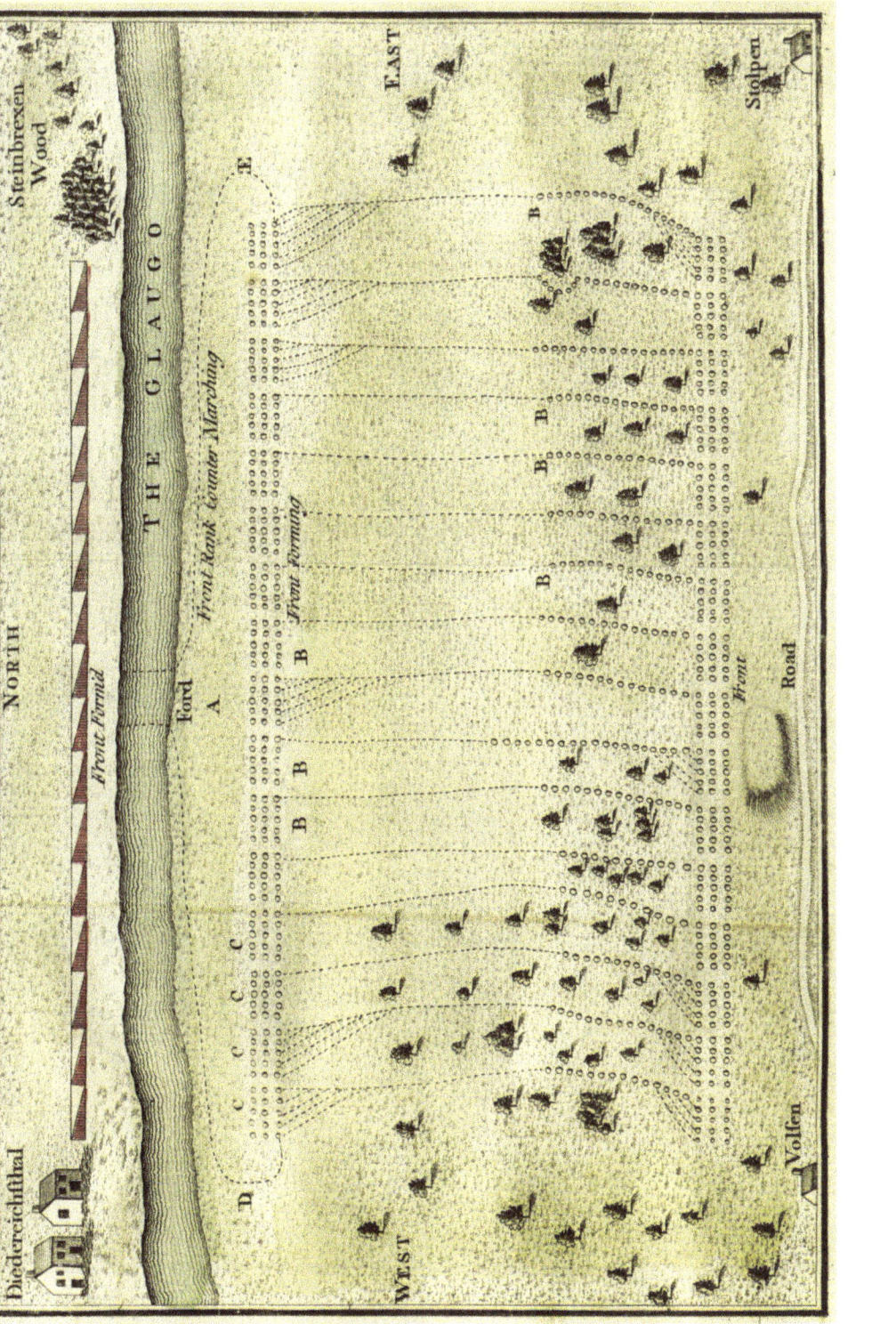

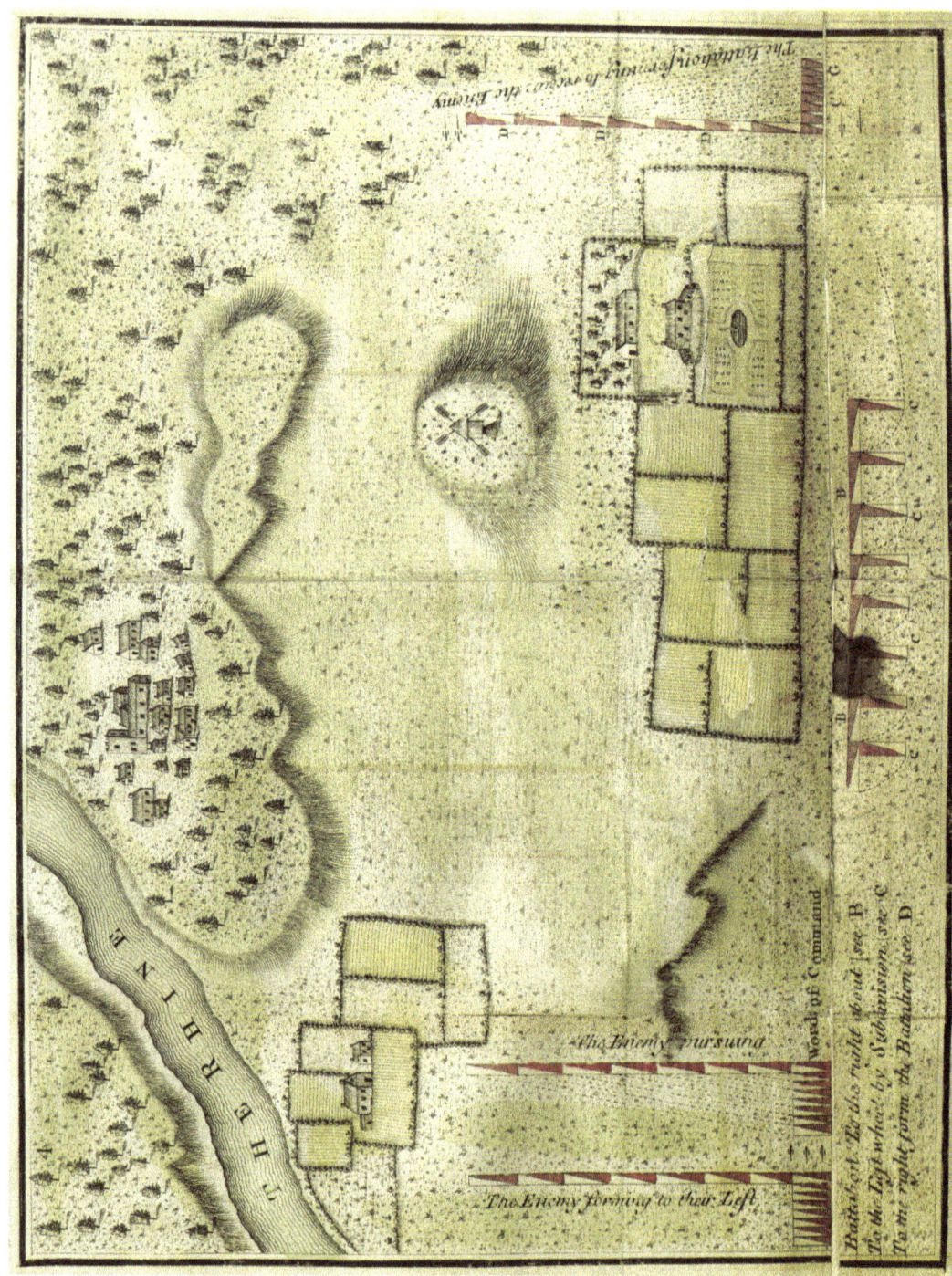

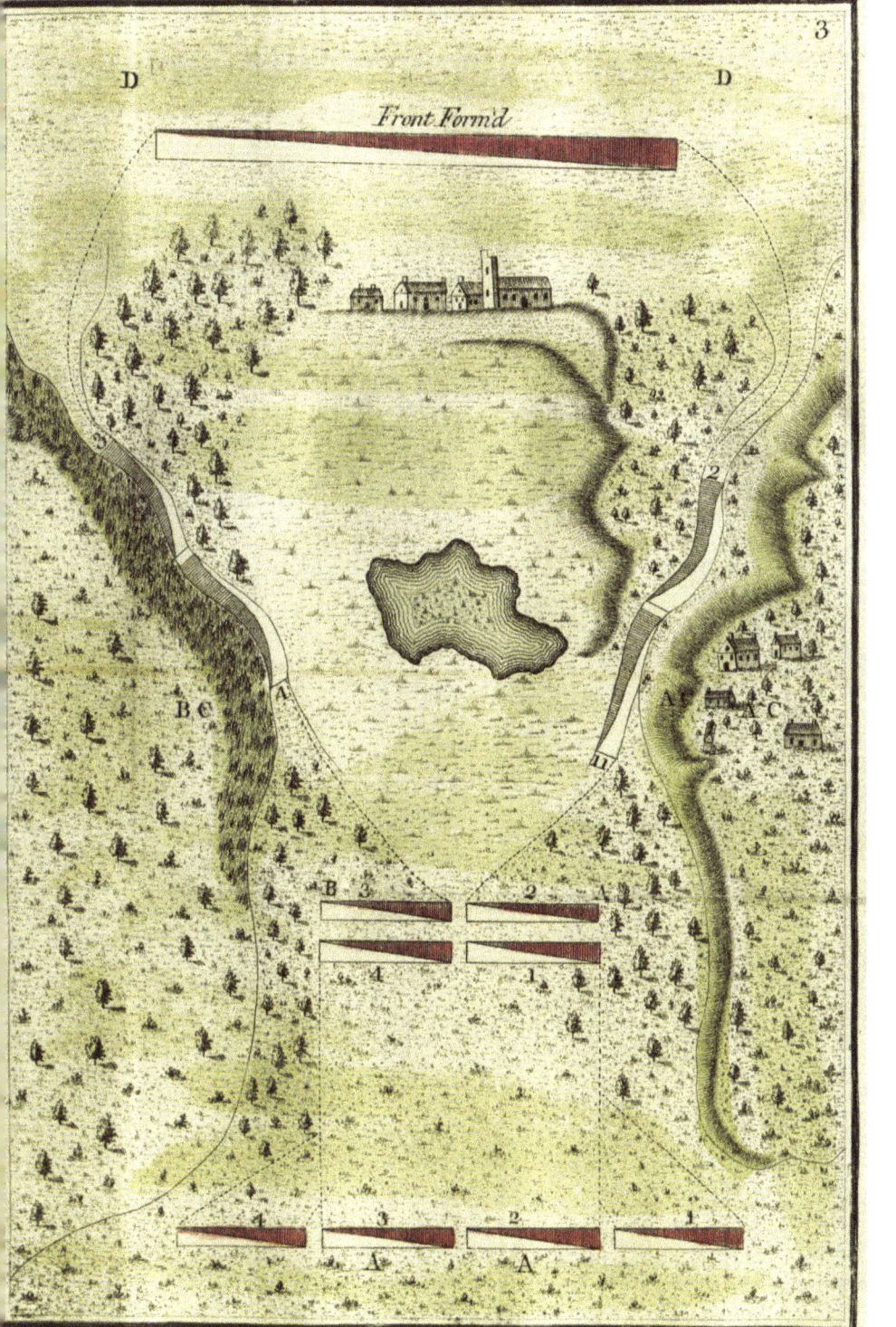

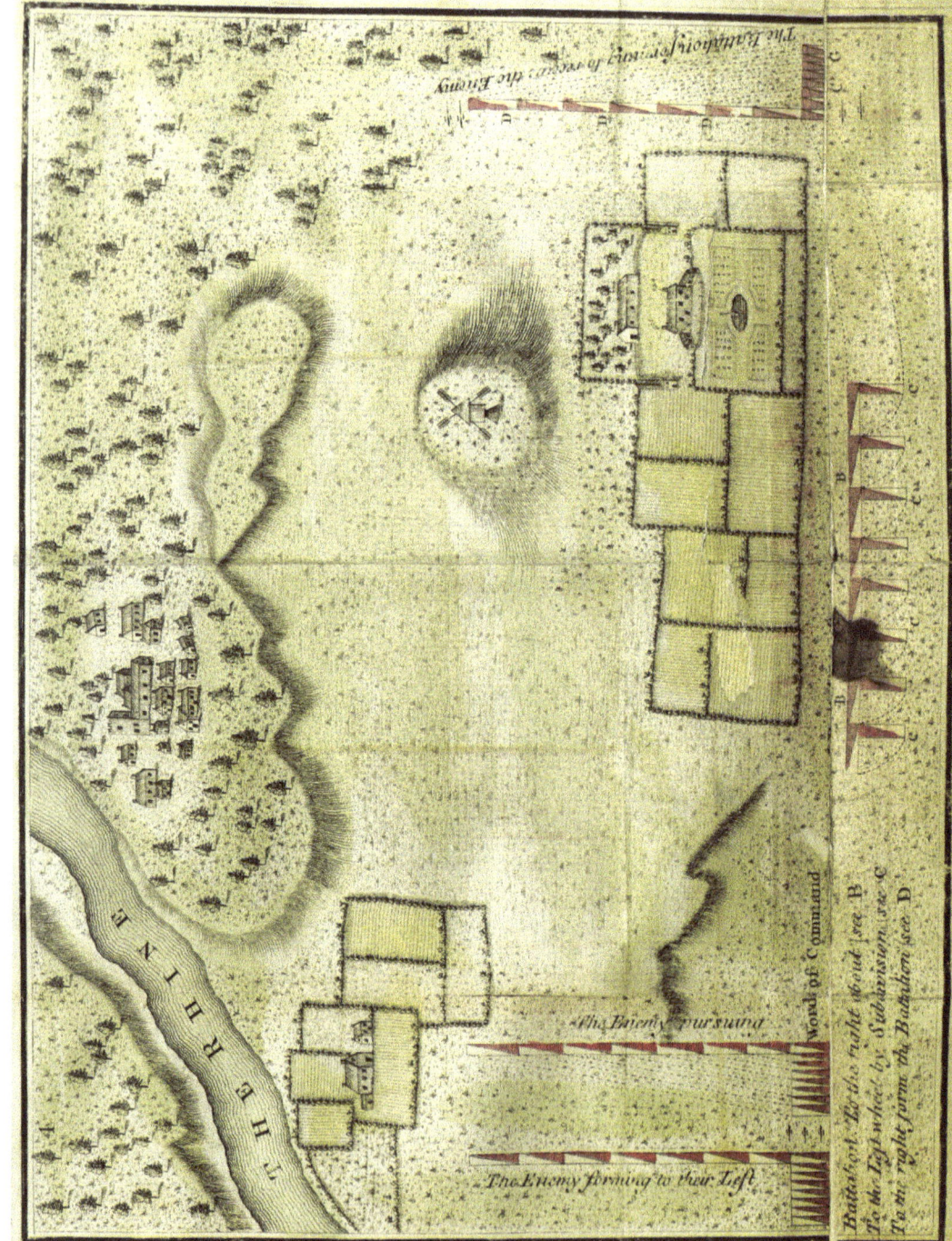

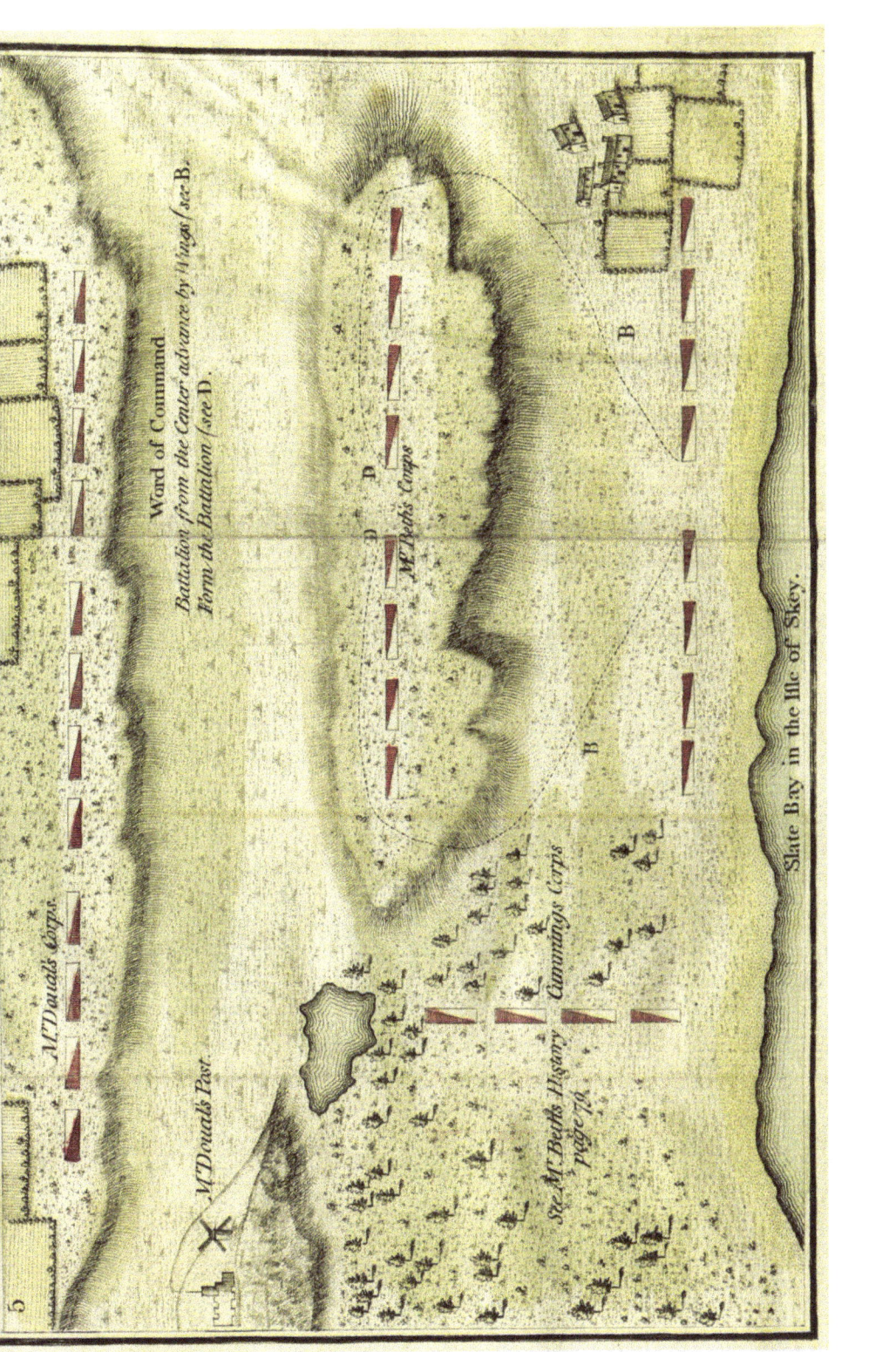

The left wing, confifting of 9. 10. 11. 12. 13. 14. 15. and 16. are moved obliquely up into the firft line; and thofe numbered 1. 2. 3. 4. 5. 6. 7. and 8. into the fecond line (fee G. H.) but before this movement was compleated, it was obferved that the antagonift inftead of endeavouring to crofs the river, was moving his battalion by files from his left, in order to pafs the bridge at K. and occupy the rifing ground from M. to N. therefore to prevent him from executing his project, which would make him mafter of the wood in the rear (marked L. N.) The following order is given (fee No. II. in the table.)

Columns! take ground to the right.

The huffars ride through the wood, N. The grenadiers following; after whom march the amufetts; while the right hand file of each grand divifion wheels to the right, the reft following in fucceffion. When the platoons are placed in this pofition, the battalion will appear with the heads of each grand divifion not equally forward; fhould it therefore be neceffary from the antagonift's *movement* to force the paffage (R. marked PRACTICABLE) the following order is given.

BATTALION FORM A SOLID COLUMN!

Upon which the right hand grand divifion halts, and the reft drefs with it (fee II.) If the paffage between M. and N. is to be forced, the word given is,

Battalion turn to the front!

Then every man turns to the left, and dreffes with his grand divifion. The battalion will then be in grand divifions, led by that on the left, and brought up by the right hand grand divifion, in which FORM there is the following advantage; when it is neceffary to take up the third pofition the word given is,

Grand divisions! to the right form the battalion.
(See No. I. in the second table.)

The left grand division being nearest the enemy, remains with its front presented to him, while the others march obliquely along its rear, to the right, or they march by files, as is judged most convenient, and so FORM the battalion from R. to D. having (P. R. D.) a ravin in front. Had the right hand grand division been nearer the enemy (which is but too commonly the case in performing this manœuvre) it must have shewn its flank, and until clear of the other grand divisions, would obstruct their fire, as would all the following grand divisions till got clear of one another, in forming to the right, but had they been to form to the left, (which could not be necessary) the contrary would have happened; I therefore would recommend to young officers, especially adjutants, to be very attentive to the advantages or disadvantages that moving from the right, left, or center, may occasion, before they give the word, in manœuvring of battalions; for I have sometimes seen even skilful parade MANOEUVRERS, when on SERVICE, commit the blunder of retiring by the left, when they should have done it to the right, *et vice versa*; and of advancing a column from the flanks, when it should have advanced from the center; and of many other errors which seem of little importance, as indeed is the case *when a battalion is not attacked*: The only inconveniency is, that some platoons may march over more ground than is necessary, in order to form; but should a battalion be attacked under these disadvantages, some confusion at least must ensue, and the principal intention of manœuvres is to avoid any confusion whatever.

Example 2d, Plate II.

DESCRIPTION.

Let there be marked upon the right of the table or east, the village of Stolpen; and on the left of it or west, the village of Volsen, to the north of which in front, is a brushwood country, bordering the river Glaugo, fordable only at A.

POSITION.

Our battalion is posted with its right at Volsen, and left at Stolpen, fronting the south, where the antagonist places two battalions, in order to attack with a superior force.

As it is necessary to retire through the brushwood country, where a file can't march a breast; the following order is given (see in the table No. I.)

Platoons! from the left retire by Indian files.

The battalion goes to the right about, and those files which were the left, (now the right) of each platoon advance, marching through the wood, followed by the other files of their platoons (see B.)

When the heads of these sixteen columns or rather ranks, arrive at the Glaugo, the word given is,

Form the battalion!

The leading files halt, (see C. in the plate) the remaining files of each platoon, move up upon its left, until the whole battalion is formed, and then the word given is,

Front!

Upon which the battalion turns to the right about, for it should always be observed that when the word *front* is given, the battalion's front rank faces the enemy, not but that a battalion may engage the enemy with its rear rank presented to him, which if composed of the shortest men would answer better, (see WOLFE, page 39) unless it is supposed that tall men are braver than short; (see VAUBAN) yet a battalion being under the necessity of engaging with its rear rank to the front, throws a slur upon the commanding officer, as it shews he has made a *false manœuvre*.

The last mentioned part of the foregoing manœuvre is done in opposition to the 4th principle of manœuvring, which says, *That even in retreats when the battalion is ordered to form, every movement should be progressive.* The reason of which maxim is, that the troops may not receive any shot in their rear while forming, which is not applicable to the present position, for if the enemy had pursued close through the wood by Indian files, the battalion would not have formed so close to the river, thereby giving up the wood in front, from which it must have been greatly awed, as sometimes has been the case *with other battalions*; but it would have formed at the edge of the wood, by the words of command.

Battalion! to the right about.

The files go to the right about, and the leading file halt.

Platoons! to the right form the battalion.
(See table 2d, No. I.)

The files in the rear incline to the right, and dress with the files which halted. (see A.)

Should the enemy move through the wood in Indian files, with one battalion, while he moves the other to attack the flanks, it will be necessary to pass the river at the ford. (see A.)

This manœuure I have seen done by some regiments, by ordering the battalion to the right about, and face to the centre, from which they march over the ford in one column, without reflecting, that from the time of commencing this manœuvre, until its completion upon the other side of the river, the part passed would not give any assistance to the part of the battalion not yet passed the ford; whereas, had the maucœuvre been begun from the flanks, these flanks when passed over the ford, could by a cross fire protect that part of the battalion not passed, in its retreat over the river; therefore the word should be,

Bat-

Battalion! from the flanks, retire by files.
(See No. II. in the table.)

The left file of the left flank, counter marches to the left, and the leading file of the right flank of the battalion countermarches to the right, followed by the others of their respective wings, meeting at the ford marked A. in plate 2d, and marching over it six in front, after passing the river, the leading file of the left wing, followed by the files of its wing, wheel to the right, and marches to the wood of Steinbrexen, on the left fronting the river, and in the same manner the leading file of the right wing marches to Diedereichthal, and without waiting the word, *form the battalion*, each officer as he arrives with his platoon upon the flanks, orders the men to front and keep up a cross fire over the river, for the protection of that part of the battalion not then passed. It requires some exactness in the officers who lead the flanks of the battalion, to judge of the distance they are to leave between them, for the rest to form in: but should they be mistaken in not giving room enough, it is not of great consequence, as the centre platoons may fall into the rear, to avoid confusion. It may even be necessary to strengthen the rear of the centre in this manner, should the enemy endeavour to pass at the ford; but for this very reason the contrary error should carefully be avoided, as it would be very dangerous to leave a weak centre exposed at the ford.

EXAMPLE III.

That the young practitioner may have an opportunity of exerting his genius, I shall describe some ground without giving a plan.

DESCRIPTION.

A battalion is drawn up on the beach of Havre de la Houle, near St. Maloes, and is ordered to ascend the hill by the narrow spoiled road, on which not more than one man can pafs abreaft. The words are, (fee table No. I.)

Battalion! from the right advance in Indian files.

The right hand file of the battalion marches forward, followed by the others in a ftring. When it is arrived upon the plain ground, on the top of the hill, it halts, the next forms upon its left, and fo on, until the whole platoon is formed, when the officer orders the platoon to reft and order, until all the fucceeding platoons are formed, and the battalion of courfe is drawn up ready to receive the enemy.

Let us now fuppofe that the country in front is not to be marched over in line, but that there are four roads made by openings in the hedges, parallel to one another; fhould the battalion march by thefe openings in four grand divifions, it is evident it fooner will be FORMED, than if ordered to march in one column by files, and this FORM will likewife occafion lefs fatigue to the men, and lefs diforder, on account of the fhortnefs of the rear; therefore the word is, (fee No. III. in the table.)

Grand Divifions! to the right advance by files.

The right hand file of each grand divifion wheels to the left, followed by the others fucceffively, and then march into the country by the openings made. When it is neceffary to form upon arriving on the plain, the word given is,

Form the battalion!

Upon which, each platoon turns to the left and wheels to the right, fo that the battalion will then be in four columns, a platoon in front of each, and if the leaders of columns have preferved their proper diftances in marching, and the heads of them are in one line, the battalion will be juftly formed, fo foon as the leading platoons halt, and the others march obliquely to the left and drefs with them.

Sup-

Suppose now that a country covered with corn presents itself to view, it is well known that if the battalion marches in line, the men will be greatly fatigued, the labour of trampling it down being incessant; but if it marches in columns, the heads of these may be relieved from time to time, and by such marching the battalion may be more or less quickly formed, according to the form prescribed; whether by wings, sub-divisions, or platoons; but it must always be observed that whatever you gain by quickly forming, you lose by fatiguing the men; an observation that may with propriety be applied to mechanical as well as military studies. The form that will least fatigue the men, is that of marching the battalion in one single column by files, through standing corn, but then the battalion, when ordered to FORM, will perform the manœuvre very slowly. Let us then chuse a medium between this, and that of marching in many columns, from the table No. III.

Wings! from the right advance by platoons.

The right hand platoon of each wing advances, the rest of the platoons incline to the right and cover it.

When these two platoons in front are a little fatigued with trampling down the corn, they turn to the right in order to let the column pass; then they turn to the left and follow the column. In this manner each of the other platoons may be relieved from the fatigue of trampling down the corn. Should the right hand platoons be at the head when the battalion is ordered to FORM, they halt while the rest inclining to the left, dress; but should they be in the rear at that instant, the forming retrograde is necessary, though contrary to the 4th principle of manœuvres, for the whole must come to the right about, incline to the right and dress; when again they go to the right about to face the enemy.

If

If this method is thought too complex, the manœuvre may be performed, adhering to the 4th principle at the same time, by the word,

Grand Divisions from the right advance by files.
(See No. II.)

The right hand file of each grand division wheels to the left, followed by the others in four columns, and when the front file of each grand division is fatigued they may fall into the rear alternately, without occasioning any difficulty when the battalion is ordered to

FORM !

Which is done by turning to the left, wheeling to the right by platoons, marching obliquely to the left, and dressing.

The battalion has now got through the standing corn, is formed upon a plain, in front of which is a *Landwher* or boundary of a grafs chaff, such as at FONTENOY, in which is an opening or *defile*, wide enough to admit of a sub-division in front, and the enemy are drawn upon the plain beyond it, the word therefore is, (see No. IV.)

Battalion from the centre advance by platoons.

The two centre platoons with the colours march forward through the defile and halt, the platoons of the right wing incline to to the left, and those of the left to the right covering each other as they march, and composing a single column of a sub-division in front.

When they have passed the defile, the platoons of the right wing incline to the right, and those of the left incline to the left, and as they severally arrive upon their ground, they dress with those formed, without waiting for the word.

Form the battalion.

The enemy now endeavour to attack the right flank. We observe that a thick wood in our front inclining to the right, at the distance of forty yards,

yards, prevents us forming the battalion to the right in order to oppose him; yet there is room enough for a grand division in front, therefore look for No. V. under C. and you'll find the manœuvre is,

Grand Division to the right change your front.
(See table II.)

The platoons of each grand division, incline to the left and dress with their respective grand divisions. The right hand grand division will be the first attacked, as it composes the front line; if it is beat, it retires by sub-divisions, round the flanks of the others, as each do in their turn, forming again in the rear.

But having pursued the enemy through the village, let us suppose that the country before us is enclosed.

The grand divisions turn to the right and follow each other in files, until we again come into an open country, we then have three different ways of forming; the first is,

To the right form the Battalion.
(See I. under C. table II.)

The second is,
To the left form the battalion.
(See table II.)

But in each of these cases the battalion would either be entirely upon the right or left of the causeway, therefore wheeling the battalion upon its centre is necessary; which manœuvre every body knows is impracticable, except upon a bowling-green; however in the following manner the battalion will form as quickly, and with less disorder. (See I. under B and 6 under C. in table I.)

Battalion on the centre to the right change the front.

The leading wing goes to the right about, the two wings will then front contrary ways; there all the platoons wheel to THEIR right, as they then front; and immediately march obliquely to the left, and dress; the right wing then comes to the right about; thus this manœuvre is performed without wheeling a longer LINE than the front of a single platoon; an object which has always been in view, while these manœuvres were composing. Suppose then we enter into an inclosed country, the road through which, only admits of a file in front, and that as we advance the road turns broad enough for a subdivision, while it opens into a plain, covered with the enemy's light troops, who are commonly so fond of baggage that it will be necessary to secure it by a proper manœuvre. The French who are never at a loss for words of embellishment from their *Colonne de Retraite*, but in a very bungling manner. We form the oblong which is done three different ways, to distinguish which the words in the table are varied by making use of the words *Advancing, Retiring, on the march*, the two first are made use of when it advances or retires in line, and the last, when at the instant of forming the oblong, the battalion is marching from the right or left by files, and as that is now supposed to be the case the word is,

Battalion! on the march form the oblong.

(See 1 under B. and 10 under C.)

If the road is not broad enough for a sub-division, the two leading platoons wheel to the right, and cover each other, until the road permits the marching of a subdivision in front, the right hand subdivisions marching in file, incline to the right of the road, and the left hand sub-divisions incline to the left, leaving the road clear in the middle, for the artillery and baggage; they then march up close, to fill up the intervals of their respective wings, when the platoons of the rear turns to the right, and wheels to the left, so that the front rank of every part of the oblong is next the enemy, which preserves the beauty of a movement.

It was this manœuvre which gained FOUQUET so much honour when he made his famous retreat from

from Kremfitz with six companies of grenadiers in presence of NADASTI, who commanded a considerable body of light troops.

EXAMPLE IV. Plate III.

Let us suppose a battalion in a plain, in front of which is an inclosed country, with an opening large enough to admit half a battalion in front, and that on the otherside there are some regiments of cavalry drawn up, upon a plain ready to make their way through this opening in order to extend their front upon the plain where our battalion is supposed to be placed, (see Plate III. A.

The battalion may remain upon the plain to receive the cavalry, which they certainly will repulse by the following difpofition. The front rank kneels, their firelocks unloaded to prevent the temptation of levelling) the butt end of the firelocks are so placed in the ground opposite the right knee, that the bayonets are presented to the enemy at an angle of 45 degrees nearly. The centre and rear ranks having their firelocks loaded. When the cavalry CHARGE they will stake their horses upon the bayonets of the front rank; and provided the infantry of that rank continue firm, the centre and rear ranks may pick of the dragoons at pleafure.

POST's Hanoverian regiments at Crevelt, defeated what the French call their beft troops, and that without loss, by the method above mentioned.

Upon the ground already described, the infantry may be *strengthened*, by forming in two lines to receive the cavalry, the first of which will be broke through if received with the whole ranks ftanding, but the second will only have to do with fquadrons in diforder.

Battalion from the centre advance by grand divisions.
(See 1 under B. and 4 under C. in the table.)

The two centre grand divisions march out to the front, the right hand grand divifion inclines or turns

turns to the left, and the left grand division inclines or turns to the right, until they join and form a second line and so occupy the space between the woods, sending their grenadiers into them to protect their flanks against their enemy's chasseurs.

As the country becomes more inclosed upon advancing, and that there are only two roads in front for the battalion to pass the swamp in its front, each of which will only admit of a file in front, the grand division marked 2 (Plate III) turns to the left and marches up the right hand road marked A. C. followed by the right hand division marked 1. and the right hand grand division of the left wing marked 3, turns to the right and marches up the road marked B. C. on the left, followed by the left hand division of that wing marked 4, from which columns the battalion is formed, upon their joining on the open ground marked D. D. For this Manœuvre the word is,

Wings from the centre advance by files!
(See Table 2 B. to 2 C.)

To shew that the ORDER OF MARCH of an Army, and the MANOEUVRING of a battalion depend upon the very same principles, though different words are used in the execution: I have adapted to the same plate, the march M'Beth is supposed to have executed in the isle of Skey, as described in the 79th page of his history, and a battalion in sub-divisions advancing from its centre, by the words,

Battalion from the centre advance by Wings.
(See plate V.)

Upon which the battalion turns to the centre, the right wing marches out by its left; and the left wing by its right. When ordered to form, all that is necessary is, that the heads of the columns do join, and the battalion then turns to its front.

Now

Now suppose the sub-divisions to be regiments, the execution of the manœuvre would have been the same, though the words are different; it would have been given out in orders, " That the right " wing of the army shall march by the left, led by " ———'s regiment &c. and the left wing shall " march by the right, led by ———'s regiment, " &c. having such and such guides, &c. &c."

As there is a description of a country given without a plan, that young gentlemen may amuse themselves in sketching it, so there is a plan (Plate IV.) given without a description, that they may describe the manœuvre by proper words of command from the table; here they are at liberty to shew their genius in forming new tables. It is not uncommon to hear the order, *Battalion! from the right advance by sub-divisions by files*, when it should simply be,

Sub-Divisions! from the right advance by files.
(See B. 4 to C. 2 in the table.)

Upon which general order, the leaders of sub-divisions march out to the front, followed by their companies, so that when the word given is,

Sub-Divisions! to the right form the battalion.
(See table II. for 2 under B. and 1 under C.

The leaders of sub divisions order their companies to turn to their left and march obliquely to the right and dress, thereby avoiding explanations from the commanding officer, as it seems to suppose that the officers did not know what were the *particular* orders to be given to their companies. How ridiculous would it appear were a general in chief, after having ordered the army to march by its right and left in ——— columns, to give particular orders that such and such regiments were to face to the right, and such to the left, and turning to the right and left march out by the roads? &c. yet are not *explanations* from a commanding officer of the same nature?

I shall conclude by giving a table still more concise than that already delineated, and perhaps as useful though it does not contain the same number of manœuvres. and to avoid increasing the number of plates, shall illustrate its use by applying it to the plates of the manœuvres published in the year 1767.

A general Table of MANOEUVRES.

B.			C.
1. Batt!	M. on the centre		1. Ind. files
2. Wings!		d. advance in	2. files
3. G. Div!	F. from the right	e. retire in	3. platoons
4. S. Div!		change	4. sub div.
5. Platt!	G. from the left	the front &	5. g. div.
6. Files!		h. form	6. wings.
7. I. Files!	N. from the flanks		7. battalion

P L A T E I.
B. 7, f = d, 3, C.

Indian Files! to the right advance in Platoons.

EXPLANATION.

See under B. for 7, and you'll find the word *Indian files*, and under C. for 3, and you'll find *plattoons*, read the intermediate words which will give the word of command above recited.

P L A T E II.

Represents a brushwood country, through which a battalion is to retire in Indian files. Suppose then the commanding officer is reconnoitring in front, and that he finds it necessary for the battalion to retire speedily through the brushwood country, yet chuses himself to remain in front, though he dare not trust his orderly huzzar with a written order, or his aid de camp with a verbal message, therefore

therefore he sends a card to the major, if commanding officer of a battalion only, or to the major of brigade if commanding a brigade or corps, upon which is wrote

B. 7, f, = e, 3, C.

When he looks at his table for 7 under B, he finds *Indian files*; for f, he finds *right*; for e, he finds *retire*; and for 3 under C. he finds *platoons*; therefore the order is, *Indian files from the right retire in platoons:* or if a corps or brigade, the order is given out by the major of brigade to the respective commanders of regiments accordingly, as regulated by the grand manœuvre *; and when he wants the battalion or brigade to form to the right he writes,

B. f, 7, = b, 7, C.

Which is, *Indian files to the right form the battalion.*

It is upon this principle that the only sure cypher is composed, as every other kind may be decyphered with time and patience; therefore to amuse the young practitioner in a part of his duty, which he must know, should he ever gain the confidence of the commander of a corps or garrison besieged: I need only give the letters referring him to the plates, that he may make out the order from the table, which will teach him its use, and the rudiments of decyphering.

PLATE III.

For the $\begin{cases} \text{manœuvre B, 5 f. 8, C.} \\ \text{PLATE V.} \\ \text{manœuvre} \end{cases}$ B. $\begin{cases} 6, \text{f. d, 5,} \\ 3, \text{g. h, 7,} \end{cases}$ C.

To form

* An example of which is here given to shew the affinity, and that the cypher of a table for the one may be made use of to ascertain the march of the other.

PLATE

(32)

Plate VI.

For the manœuvre B.{ 6, g. d, 5, } C.
To form -   { 3, g. h, 7, }

That is, Grand Divisions! to the left form the battalion.

Plate IX.

For the manœuvre B.{ 6, f. e, 6, } C.
To form - -   { 2, g. h, 7, }

Plate X.

B, 3 { f.=d, 3, C. Forming, B, 5, g.=h, 7, C.

Plate XI.

{ f.=8, C. coloured red in the plate,
  B, 3, g.=h, 8, C. coloured green.

Plate XII.

B, 5, f.=e, 6, C. coloured red. B, 2, g.=h, 7, C. coloured green.

Plate XIII.

B, 6, m.=d, 6, C. . . . B, 2, m.=h, 7, C.

Plate XIV.

B, 6, m.=e, 6, C. that is, Files from the flanks retire in *wings*.

B, 2, m.=h, 7, C. that is, *Wings! on the centre form the battalion.*

By which means we constantly begin the order to *form* with the word the manœuvre ended in, that the battalion may always be spoke to in the form they are marching in, which is the intention of this table.

Plate V. (but supposed retiring.)

A brigade composed of four battalions is so encamped, that it can retire through the openings made in the hedges, in four columns, and that the brigadier general with the right troops being in front, finds himself so hard pressed, that it's necessary to retire in four columns. Suppose likewise, that he cannot trust a huzzar with a written order,

or his aid-de-camp with a verbal message, and that he writes to his major of brigade upon a card,
B, 5, f. = e, 2, C.

Upon receiving which the major of brigade, reads from the table, *Platoons! from the right retire in files*; but as he is an officer of the general staff, he applies this regimental order to the *grand manœuvre*, where opposite to the word *platoons*, he will find the word *battalions*, therefore he will order the *battalions to retire from the right by files*. And then they march to the rear by the different roads allotted them having their guides, &c. &c. &c.

But how trifling is even the *grand manœuvre*, which only regulates the march and forming of an army, when compared to the other duties of a great general, whose knowledge of the country, though a science that requires the greatest abilities, is not inferior to his foresight in providing for the subsistance of his army. When we reflect upon the great and sublime qualities that are necessary to constitute the character of a commander in chief, we should implicitly obey, and chearfully execute his orders.

FINIS.

www.ingramcontent.com/pod-product-compliance
Ingram Content Group UK Ltd.
Pitfield, Milton Keynes, MK11 3LW, UK
UKHW022328240426
12048UKWH00052B/665